Fighting Disease, Not Death:

Finding a way through lifelong struggle

By Lorie L. and Mark L. Vincent
Foreword by Paul J. LeMarbre, M.D.

www.DesignGroupInternational.com

Cover photo by Sonya Richards

First published by Dog Ear Publishing
4010 W. 86th Street, Ste H
Indianapolis, IN 46268
www.dogearpublishing.net

ISBN: 978-145750-460-0

This book is printed on acid-free paper.

Printed in the United States of America

Dedication

We dedicate this book to anyone diagnosed with leiomyosarcoma and their families. May you know the full measure of a life well lived. Kathy, Bev and Kathy. . . you did.

The only young woman I love
The one who fits like a glove
Has broken her lung
But her song is not sung
So breathe deep and sing,
   Raven-haired dove
Breathe deep and sing,
   Raven-haired dove.

The only young woman for me
She whom I keep company
Is dying somewhere
Cause she can't breathe the air
But breathe deep and sing,
   Raven-haired dove
Breathe deep and sing,
   Raven-haired dove.

This lovely young woman I've known
Has put love deep in my bones.
Don't know what will come
Or where it will come from
But I'll breathe deep and sing,
   Raven-haired dove
I'll breathe deep and sing,
For my raven-haired dove.

mark l vincent - 2001

ACKNOWLEDGEMENTS

Our faith in God as one who is both sovereign and near to our individual circumstance runs deep. We have our parents and grandparents to thank for this because they didn't teach us to be superstitious or magical in our spiritual lives, but practical and real.

Faith for us is an everyday exercise of placing trust in God that we are part of a larger design. The more we learn about it, the more we learn there is an eternal vastness of what remains to be known. Our young adult children were forced to grow up while watching their mother suffer. They shared the agony of some of our medical decisions and were forced to worry about what life would be like without her. They are sensitive, serving and wise beyond their years as a result. We think this growth is part of the larger design beyond our own circumstance. Besides, who are we to think cancer is an unmanageable problem when we have been granted so many extra years together?

We are especially grateful for the deep love of so many family members—our parents especially, friends, and even people who only know a bit about our story. Their prayers and expressions of encouragement are beyond number and give us strength along the way—time and again. Chief among them are Brian and Vickie Van de Water, Lorie's sister and husband. They and their children embraced us into their lives and community at a time everyone thought Lorie had just a few months to live. For ten years, they gave, loved and shared life with us, facing the ugliness and stress of a long battle with cancer beside us.

And how do we even begin to say thank you to Dr. Paul LeMarbre and the nurses and staff of ProHealth Care at the Regional Cancer Centers in Mukwonago and Waukesha, Wisconsin? In a world where medical professionals have many competing pressures to make medicine a secondary mission, they are stalwart and heroically committed to patient care. It was Dr. LeMarbre who asked us to try yet one more thing when all the other doctors said it was time to call hospice. Our children agreed even if it meant Lorie's life was at even greater risk. "You have to try!" they said. That was now eleven years ago, wonderful, precious extra years to love and serve…together.

-Lorie L. and Mark L. Vincent

Table of Contents

FOREWORD

Cancer is a reality in our existence as it touches the lives in various ways of virtually every human being. Just as every person is unique every cancer represents a point in a vast spectrum of differing disease states. In addition the mechanisms whereby an individual copes and hopefully succeeds in overcoming this dreaded condition vary widely. So much can be learned in a situation where we face our own mortality or the mortality of someone dear to us. This opportunity to change physically, emotionally, and spiritually carries with it the potential to fulfill the meaning of our lives not only to ourselves but also to those around us. Individuals facing cancer often exhibit courage, honesty, determination and an appreciation for the love that surrounds them. For some however the opportunity is lost as fear, anger, pessimism and hopelessness dominate the moments of those caught in the struggle.

There are and will be accounts of remarkable individuals who overcome the burden of cancer either by achieving a remission (even a cure) or who bear an inescapable illness with such beautiful dignity and humility that they inspire those around them. This book relates one such marvelous story—a story I know to be true having witnessed it for most of its entirety. Lorie and Mark Vincent tell us of the events and feelings they have experienced as they found their way through Lorie's struggle with a rare and deadly cancer. In a clear and frank style they tell of the emotions and lessons of their cancer experience—in addition they offer us their insights into the spiritual foundations that provide them with the strength and resilience to turn a difficult experience into an unforgettably positive chapter in their lives. As I have had the privilege of coming to know these two rare human beings I am reminded of one of life's finest concepts: in our search for God we have only to truly look at and cherish the other human souls around us for God will be present in them, and hopefully we will recognize the same gift in ourselves.

- Paul J LeMarbre MD
2011

INTRODUCTION

We began writing because so many people asked us to preserve our story in some way. The challenge was how to do so and what approach to take. So many found Lorie's story to be inspiring but one does not have to spend a lot of time in a bookstore to find yet another sensational and inspirational story. A second possible approach would be advice for those battling cancer, but better advice than we could give already exists. Furthering conversation about how a Christian approaches suffering was also a possibility, but we wondered whether yet another book on faith in the midst of suffering was needed. We mentioned these reservations to several of those urging us to write. What ultimately convinced us to begin was their suggestion it would be unique to combine all three themes. Instead of trying to decide which sort of book to write, or writing three separate books, why not just write one that combined them? Our friends believed it was our approach—our experience, our beliefs, and ultimately our method—that made it important to put it into words. We began developing the idea.

Interestingly, as we mapped out what we wanted to say, what initially felt like crushing three books into one became the simplest of outlines and what we now consider to be a profound statement of choosing to live. Our convictions of how to approach suffering that shows up in our lives were strengthened by putting our approach into words. We pray it also benefits you.

It is not whether a person defies the odds and avoids pain that defines success. Could such a person even be considered fortunate since she or he would be both insensitive and ignorant of the human experience? The appropriate assumption is that everyone collects painful circumstances as they navigate their lifetimes. If we try to run away from them or deny their existence, we deprive ourselves of lessons we might learn and gifts we might receive. If we surrender to them, the pain crushes us and we die before we are dead. If we are blindly angered by what hurts us, we lash out and become the source of painful memories in others' lives. Instead, it is what sort of platform we build upon pain and suffering that marks human triumph. We choose again and again to build a platform of achievement in worship of the God who made us.

Rather than write this book entirely in first or third person, we chose to switch back and forth, depending on whether a particular passage reflects both or just one of our voices. This may feel a little strange to one's reading ear at first, but the switching back and forth quickly fades into the background and keeps the story moving.

We open with our family and Lorie's cancer. We then describe how our faith developed and how it enabled us to face long term and debilitating disease. Chapters three through five describe other choices a person might make when faced with similar circumstances and why we consider those approaches lacking, harmful even. We close with an appeal to join us in building platforms of praise on the circumstances of our lives. We welcome your reflections on what you read here. Feel free to contact us at: info@designgroupintl.com.

CHAPTER ONE

It's not a chapter, it's the book!

"You don't have cancer anymore" …a strange way to be told you have it in the first place. Lorie was lying in a hospital bed in 1999, recovering from an overdue hysterectomy, when her gynecologist entered the room and made the announcement.

There was no suspicion Lorie had cancer. The doctor never said what type of cancer it was, only that it was gone, the surgical margins were clear and that nothing further needed to be done. She later resisted our request for a second opinion. Looking back, we think she knew just how rare, dangerous and untreatable the cancer was. We wonder if she wanted us to have an enjoyable life until the cancer returned. The alternative that she was ignorant of this type of cancer is too frightening to think about.

We were naive enough to believe this was good news. We phoned our family to tell them of the successful surgery and the major scare we escaped. Lorie's mother was a career nurse in Sheboygan, Wisconsin, whose office was across the hall from a pathologist. Lorie had already argued with her about the need for a second opinion, which Lorie dismissed as pessimism, but Lorie agreed she could discuss it with him. This was the first time we took a good look at the specific name of the cancer found in Lorie's uterine lining. *Leiomyosarcoma*. The pathologist immediately confirmed it was deadly. Lorie needed to see an oncologist immediately.

Now frightened into wanting more information we began searching. Mark corresponded with a University of Chicago physician who confirmed that leiomyosarcoma in any form had no five year survival rates. Lorie's cancer was rare—so rare that many oncologists would never see a case, so rare it was difficult to create cohorts of patients for study, and so rare no medicines were specifically targeted for it. The only hope he gave us was that if it had been caught early enough perhaps no metastasis would take place. He recommended Lorie be scanned every six months for three years. He said it would not take that long, however. If it came back it would be in less than two years and it would reoccur in her lungs.

The cancer reoccurred eighteen months later—a great big tumor in Lorie's right lung.

During those eighteen months we found an oncologist in South Bend. We also saw a gynecological oncologist and a radiation oncologist who confirmed everything we learned from Mark's conversation with the University of Chicago physician. All we could do was wait, scan every so often, and hope it never came back. As far as the medical community was concerned, chemotherapy used in leiomyosarcoma cases never extended anyone's life beyond five years, even if tumors shrank from the treatment. Radiation was also worthless. They believed it might actually accelerate tumor growth.

Our hopes increased that Lorie was of the rare and fortunate few with each subsequent clear scan. So, it was difficult news to hear that half of Lorie's right lung was consumed with a significant and rapidly growing tumor when just six months earlier the scan showed nothing but healthy lungs.

We learned the news on a Wednesday. The following Monday half of Lorie's right lung was removed. Recovery lasted six months. The doctors felt Lorie might have another twelve to eighteen months before the cancer would return yet again, this time with nothing more to be done.

This first reoccurrence and subsequent thoracotomy and lung resection took place in the spring of 2001. Lorie was 37 years old. Our children were 11 and 13. We had just started the consulting firm Design Group International™ and listed and received an offer on our house, preparing to move to Arizona where Mark was candidating at Sunnyslope Mennonite Church. They had recruited him to come as a part-time Senior Pastor and to bring mentoring leadership to a pastoral team they wanted to form, thus leaving him free to pursue some of the innovative organizational development and stewardship education projects he had been pioneering. Our life had been moving forward at an exciting, meaningful and fulfilling pace.

We will never forget that Wednesday when we got the news. If Lorie wanted to live longer than a few months she needed an immediate and incredibly invasive surgery. Our children were still in school when we came home from meeting with the oncologist. We sat on our couch, drained and afraid. We began talking through our options and fell asleep in mid-conversation. We since learned we both have the same stress reaction, the exhaustion of it puts us to sleep.

We didn't sleep long. When we awakened we were refreshed and somehow knew the course we should take. If Lorie had just a few remaining months, she wanted to spend whatever time she had near her family in Wisconsin. She was especially concerned about her sister Vickie who was recently married after a difficult first marriage, her niece, Erica and her newest nephew, Hunter. Lorie wanted to invest in these relationships before she died.

There was weeping at both ends of the phone line when we informed Sunnyslope's Search Committee that we could not pursue the candidacy. Our son was the most devastated among us as he was cheering for all the Phoenix professional sports teams in anticipation of living in the Valley of the Sun.

Ten days after Lorie's surgery, her grandmother died. She was devastated not to be physically strong enough to make the trip for the funeral as she had just been released from the hospital. Mark's sister, Gina, and her family, came to stay with her while Mark and our children traveled to Wisconsin for the funeral. Before coming home, Lorie's sister Vickie helped Mark, Autumn and Zach shop for a home in Wisconsin. The goal was to find a home where someone could die peacefully and where a single father could finish raising his family. We purchased a home in the woods a couple of miles from Vickie's family. By June all of us were newly located in Mukwonago, Wisconsin. We were able to complete this abrupt transition only because both our parents, siblings, extended families and church family at Belmont Mennonite Church in Elkhart, Indiana provided a lot of help. Mark's parents, especially, travelled north from Florida multiple times to help Mark get the house ready.

The summer of 2001 was pretty quiet. Lorie got stronger with each passing week. Our children were enrolled in their new schools. We began looking for a church home. Mark traveled a bit, working with clients from our new base of operations. We had not yet found a new oncologist when it was time for the next scans of Lorie's chest, now increased to every three months. Over an extended August weekend, we traveled back to Indiana for scans and results.

While we were gone, Lorie's parents took our children and visited a congregation that our children immediately loved. Vickie's family attended that Sunday too and felt the same. They called to tell us a church home had been found hoping we would agree. The next day the oncologist told us the cancer was back, a tumor in each lung.

This second reoccurrence, just as Lorie completed her recovery from an extensive lung resection, introduced a new chapter of our journey with the disease. Everything happened as the oncologists had said: the first reoccurrence within two years, the likelihood of death before five. Now we were faced with the end game. The medical community of Northern

Indiana followed the textbook and recommended we prepare for hospice services and the journey toward death. Chemotherapy and radiation would not help. Nothing more was to be done except enjoy whatever time remained. They felt Lorie might live another six months. The next scan in October confirmed both tumors were growing rapidly. All this as our COBRA insurance was running out because our previous insurance company did not provide coverage in Wisconsin. We had to move quickly and find an oncologist in Wisconsin before year end.

We had been in Wisconsin for five months but we knew nothing about the medical community near our new home. We were surprised and pleased to discover that Waukesha Memorial, our community hospital, was a top cancer treatment facility. At least they would know something about leiomyosarcoma.

As we searched for a new oncologist, one name kept coming up: Dr. Paul LeMarbre. Trained at Dartmouth, he is a contributor to medical texts on the importance and therapeutic effects of a physician's bedside manner (*Oncology for the House Officer*, Williams and Wilkins, 1992). We were able to get an appointment with him on December 20, his last office day of 2001 in Mukwonago.

Our first meeting with him provided yet another unforgettable moment. Lorie's medical files were already quite extensive. We brought the heavy stack of films with us and Lorie told Dr. LeMarbre the whole story. He listened intently, especially as Lorie asked what his recommendations would be for the final months of her life. Perhaps he could recommend a good hospice program? His response was the first words of hope we heard from anyone: *"But you aren't ready for hospice yet. I think I can help you."*

Dr. LeMarbre felt she had an option. He had developed a treatment protocol that included MAID[1], an in-patient 96-hour continuous IV chemotherapy infusion consisting of Mesna, Doxorubicin, Ifosfamide, and Dacarbazine (DTIC). The chemotherapy, when combined with Tamoxifen, brought good results to some patients. He felt Lorie's relatively young age and otherwise healthy condition were in her favor. Lorie remained skeptical because of the many doctors in Indiana who told us leiomyosarcoma did not respond to chemotherapy. Hearing this, Dr. LeMarbre proposed that if Lorie would allow a lung biopsy to remove a small piece of the tumor, the chemotherapy could be done in the lab to see if the tumor responded. Lorie agreed to see a cardiothoracic surgeon in January to perform the biopsy and test the chemotherapy in the lab.

Armed with our new hope, we moved forward to this consultation. In preparation for the expected biopsy, new CT scans of the chest, abdomen and pelvis were ordered by Dr. Curtis Quinn. He looked at the scans before entering the exam room, expecting to be able to tell us whether or not the biopsy could be performed. He was startled by what he saw on the scans, and was certainly not prepared to deliver the news to a beautiful woman with school-aged children. What were two tumors just a few weeks before now

---

[1] The MAID protocol was published in 1989. Elias, Anthony et al; *Journal of Clinical Oncology* 7: 1208-1216, 1989

numbered more than twenty. It was as if a seed pod exploded in Lorie's lungs—and not just in her lungs. Tumors were growing in her abdomen and pelvis. A lung biopsy would do no good. Lorie's six remaining months were compressing rapidly.

Dr. Quinn could not hide his emotions as he met with us. More than once, and through his thick Boston inflection, he wondered how we could be so calm when hearing such devastating news. Our only answer then was that anger, tears, bitter resignation or demanding a doctor provide a different prognosis would be of no help. We refused to be conquered by what we could not change. We were choosing to do what was within our power to do with what little energy and time remained.

With surgery no longer an option, we returned to our new oncologist. Dr. LeMarbre admitted we now faced the direst of scenarios, but once again pointed us to a hope-filled outcome. The MAID protocol could still be pursued. It required six rounds of intense chemotherapy administered during a week of hospitalization. This protocol was likely the only treatment that could provide a fighting chance due to the cancer's aggressive and rapid progression.

Dr. LeMarbre did not mince words. This treatment might not work at all. It definitely would make Lorie sick—so sick it could take her life even sooner. Her immune system would be significantly compromised. When not hospitalized, home was the only place Lorie could be due to a high risk of infection from exposure to germs. And yet, the protocol might work.

We did not feel we could make this decision on our own. Zach was now half-way through his sixth grade year and Autumn, her eighth. We sat down for a family conversation. We did not want our children to feel the decision to proceed or not rested on their shoulders, but we wanted to inform them what was at stake and to strongly consider their opinion. We told them their mother might die even faster and that she would be ill and gone a lot of the time for the next six months. Our children did not need any time to reflect. Both of them said, "You have to try!"

Five minutes into the conversation we were resolved to proceed. Lorie's face was as that of Jesus, the proverbial flint set toward Jerusalem (Luke 9:51), she was so resolute. Lorie's mom, Marilyn, took a family medical leave of absence from nursing and agreed to come live with us to care for Lorie and our household. Don, Lorie's dad, came on the weekends to help in any way he could and gained the endearing name of *Benson* that remains to this day. This let Mark continue working and providing health insurance.

So January 2002 began a six month journey through the Valley of the Shadow of Death. Each month Lorie entered the hospital for five days of continuous infusion chemotherapy. By the third day of each treatment, Lorie went into a significant stupor that lasted up to a week beyond the treatment. Lorie was often too ill to come home right away and five days of hospitalization would turn into seven or eight.

Before the second round of chemo in February, Lorie's ebony and auburn waist-length hair began coming out. Vickie's husband, Brian, came over with his clippers to do the honors of making Lorie look like Demi Moore in the film *G.I. Jane*.

Between the second and third round, a bald, weak and extremely fatigued Lorie lay on a hospital couch, masked and gowned, as her sister Vickie gave birth to our nephew Brandon. Each time we are with this particular nephew, we are reminded that the memories our children, nephews and nieces have of Lorie is of one battling a long-term disease. They are too young to know her as anything other than the sick aunt they pray for each night when they are tucked into bed.

Before the third round of chemo, Lorie had a life-threatening infection that nearly took her. It was a horrific night of Mark holding her in the emergency room as she passed in and out of the rigors and consciousness. The infection source proved to be her double lumen Hickman catheter, though this was unknown for almost 48 hours. A potent intravenous antibiotic and an emergency removal of the catheter saved her life. Recovering from this infection, and yet another surgery to put in a BardPort®, added to the length of the protocol.

By the fourth round, Lorie's short-term memory began to fail and didn't return until the MAID Protocol ended.

It was July before it was over, but Lorie came through cancer free. All twenty-one tumors disappeared.

A few weeks later, Lorie was invited by our Pastor, Verne Hagenbeck, to share a word of testimony in the worship services of the congregation our extended family now attended. Waukesha First Assembly had held us closely in their bosom, bringing us meals several times each week for seven months. Because of this generosity, neither Marilyn nor Mark needed to worry about cooking while caring for Lorie, and we were able to keep our children on as normal a schedule as we could. Our gratitude for this expression of loving service from this congregation was boundless. How could Lorie refuse her pastor's request?

In her testimony, she described the seven months as a fog, but a holy time where she was able to bear witness to the goodness of God, using a hospital bed as her new pulpit since she could no longer work directly in local church ministry.

A new health complication arose about this time. Lorie developed a serious blood clot from the right central vena cava to the common iliac vein, probably due to the combination of lying in bed so long during the months of the MAID protocol, the MAID protocol itself, and taking Tamoxifen. The clot was life-threatening and required careful monitoring, but we were almost grateful to face this scary scenario instead of the ones we had faced already.

As Lorie began regaining strength, the cancer returned for the fourth time, in time for Christmas 2002. Lorie had just received a final treatment of maintenance chemo in mid-December when she came down with a cold and a scary cough. When she went to Urgent Care, they consulted with Dr. LeMarbre. He ordered an immediate chest CT at the hospital. It showed two tumors not there just two months before. Dr. LeMarbre suggested treating these two tumors with radiation, but since it was days before Christmas and radiation could not be set up before the first of the year, he put Lorie on a small dose of a newer chemotherapy drug called Gemzar. Though not trialed for leiomyosarcoma, Gemzar was administered in the hope of keeping the tumors from growing during the Holidays before radiation therapy could begin. With his encouragement, we followed through with our plan for a much needed and long postponed family vacation. After a morning infusion of Gemzar, we boarded a plane to Marco Island, FL for ten days of rest, card-playing and long walks on the beach with our children. We each quietly wondered if it would be our last family vacation.

******

Lorie's scans upon our return revealed a wonderful Christmas gift. The tumors shrank by half after just one treatment. Gemzar seemed an effective way to go but the problem was Gemzar and radiation therapy do not pair well. Dr. James Richardson, Lorie's Radiation Oncologist, explained that Gemzar acts like an accelerant with the radiation, potentially causing its strength to be harmful. A compromise of lowering the dose of Gemzar and making the radiation field smaller was agreed upon. The combined treatment began and after a few months the tumors were gone with minimal side effects. All involved were relieved and joyful. Dr. LeMarbre then developed a chemotherapy maintenance program for Lorie for the months beyond, gradually reducing the dosage of Gemzar after several ensuing scans remained clear. Over Easter break 2003, the week before her next monthly chemo treatment, we took a family trip to the highlands of Scotland. Autumn and Zach talk about this as the best family trip ever. We agree.

Unfortunately by September 2003, more cancer. For the fifth time. Already. This time, Lorie had a couple of rapidly growing tumors. The good news was that they could be removed surgically. The bad news was that they could be removed surgically and the recovery would again last several months. Lorie's second lung resection was scheduled. Dr. Curtis Quinn operated; glad he could be of service this time. Lorie's mom moved back in to help Mark keep the household running, this time taking early retirement.

Lorie's recovery took four months instead of the six it took the first time. In part, this was because Dr. Quinn was able to remove less lung tissue due to the location of the tumors, and because Lorie had become more fit and lost weight in the weeks after the MAID protocol had ended. By reducing her bread intake, eating whole rather than processed foods and exercising daily, she was more physically prepared for surgery than she had been previously.

Lorie's lungs remained cancer free for almost two years after the second lung resection, but not her body. A small tumor was discovered in her pelvis the summer of 2004. Radiation was used to successfully treat that tumor. As hard as it would have been if it were the original diagnosis, daily trips for radiation during Lorie's sixth occurrence of treatment for leiomyosarcoma hardly felt like an interruption in comparison to what Lorie had experienced already.

During these two years, and even with the tumor in Lorie's pelvis, life began to return to what we had long forgotten. A few of us even began to dare to breathe the word *remission*.

September 2005 brought any relief from disease to an end: more lung tumors and need for a third lung resection. Marilyn packed her bags and moved into our home to help yet again. Dr. Quinn removed minimal tissue this time because the tumors were wonderfully close to the surface. Lorie recovered in about three months and resumed her exercise to keep maximizing her constantly diminishing lung capacity, now down by about fifty percent.

While in the hospital, Lorie wore a boxer's robe Mark gave her, celebrating a victory over cancer's seventh round. Dr. Quinn loved the robe so much he reported it to the public relations office of the hospital. The story spread and became a Milwaukee television news story and even a front page item in a Sunday edition of the *Milwaukee Journal Sentinel*. More importantly, Lorie had now survived six years with cancer. She had crossed the unheard of five year threshold for a person with metastatic uterine leiomyosarcoma.

Lorie's neck bothered her immediately after the surgery. We all attributed the neck pain to the awkward positioning on the surgeon's table during the lung resection. When the pain persisted, however, Dr. LeMarbre agreed with Lorie that further examination was necessary. A scan showed a new tumor in the C2-C3 cervical spine (neck). Radiation in summer of 2006 required Dr. Richardson's best efforts in order not to cause permanent damage to Lorie's spine. This tumor, too, went away.

September 2006 brought new lung tumors and Lorie's fourth lung resection. In medical conference, some of Dr. Quinn's associates wondered whether Lorie's quality of life might not be suffering at this point. Dr. Quinn told them in no uncertain terms that they did not know his patient's stamina or will to live. Still, he felt some research was in order and triumphantly told Lorie his discovery that four lung resections was not new territory. He found a case of a woman older than Lorie who underwent seven. We all took a deep breath and entered the search, destroy and then recover zone again. Marilyn moved in once more and helped hold our home together until just before Christmas. In honor of Lorie's survival of nine occurrences of cancer, Mark gave her a statue of a lioness at rest.

We had a break of nearly a year before cancer returned in the fall of 2007. Wonderfully, Lorie had now lived long enough that a new treatment option was available: CyberKnife®. This form of radiation uses high doses of focused radiation beams to precisely treat tumors of a certain size contained within moving tissue, as in the lungs, in real time, even as the patient takes a breath with minimal damage to adjacent normal tissue. It felt like the stuff of science fiction, but it worked. Lorie became one of the first CyberKnife® patients in Southeastern Wisconsin, and one of the first ever to have CyberKnife® for treatment of leiomyosarcoma. What an improvement CyberKnife® is! Instead of broken ribs, enormous chest tubes and incisions the length of Lorie's shoulder blade, followed by months of recovery, Lorie went to Day Surgery to have gold fiducial markers placed in the tumor. They were inserted by a needle in the Interventional Radiology Department and she was released by day's end. Once a scan confirmed the fiducials remained in place, Lorie lay under the CyberKnife® machine for three hours every other day for five treatments. The only things touching her body were the electrodes to monitor her heart rate. Lorie remained completely awake as the CyberKnife® machine targeted the tumors with 180 beams of radiation that destroyed only the tumor and little else. No anesthesia, cutting, or pain! In a relatively short time it was over and life resumed.

The success of CyberKnife® led us to wonder whether leiomyosarcoma might now be treated as a chronic condition rather than a fatal diagnosis. Lorie had now survived seven years and was cancer free again after ten occurrences of this nasty and persistent disease.

Tumors were found again in July 2008. Round eleven proved to be nasty. There were five identified tumors spread throughout Lorie's lungs and not surgically approachable without removing more lung than she needed to live. There were too many tumors to be treated by CyberKnife®. We were once again faced with chemotherapy. After three months, more devastating news. The tumors were growing and a sixth tumor could be seen. Dr. LeMarbre suggested a possibility of using an angiogenesis drug in combination with chemotherapy. This new class of drugs targets the blood supply of tumors, cutting it off and killing the tumor. Of course, the drug was not designed for leiomyosarcoma, so its success would be hypothetical. Further, it was very expensive and not covered by Lorie's insurance. Fortunately for us, Genentech Medical Foundation agreed to provide the Avastin for what might be learned from Lorie's case.

The tumors stopped growing when the combination of drugs began. Over the next seven months, three tumors disappeared and the other three appeared to go dormant. The problem, however, was that courses of chemotherapy normally run six months. Lorie was now in her tenth month and she was failing noticeably. At this point the only way we could know if the three remaining tumors were dead was to stop chemotherapy and see if they grew. Lorie's vitality improved remarkably within two weeks of stopping chemotherapy, but the tumors began growing within two months. The good news was that CyberKnife® was again a possibility now that the tumors were reduced to three. Was Lorie willing to be one of the few persons in the country to repeat CyberKnife® on her lungs, as well as being one of the first at the hospital to be treated for three tumors simultaneously? Considering the alternatives, it was an easy yes to give.

CyberKnife® was not nearly so easy this time around. Lorie coughed up one of the fiducial markers so only two tumors could be treated at first. When replacing the marker for the third tumor, Lorie's lung collapsed and stubbornly refused to re-inflate. It took chest tubes of three different sizes and a week in the hospital before Lorie's lung began to hold a seal again. But by September 2009, CyberKnife® procedures were complete.

Scans in December 2009 showed all three tumors resolving. Those words were a delight to hear, along with the realization Lorie had survived ten years. She was now widely believed to be the longest lived person with metastatic uterine leiomyosarcoma.

During this December examination, Lorie asked that a lump on the side of her head and one in her knee be examined because they were growing and the one on her head was becoming painful. Dr. LeMarbre referred her to a general surgeon, Dr. Kevin Hart, who agreed with Dr. LeMarbre that they were probably benign cysts called lipomas made up of fatty tissue, but given Lorie's history and current discomfort it could be removed if she wanted. Lorie wanted.

Dr. Hart described the cyst in the knee as a lipoma, but the one in the head was "unique" and something he had "never seen before." Pathology brought back the dreaded news: the cyst in the scalp was a leiomyosarcoma metastasis. This news led to a PET scan revealing no additional cancer in Lorie's body, which meant no chemotherapy or radiation would be required if additional tissue removed from her scalp showed the surgical margins to be clear. The day after her stitches were removed the incision was reopened to remove a ping pong ball sized chunk of flesh from Lorie's scalp. Pathology showed the surgical margins to be clear. Round twelve was behind us. Dr. Hart even preserved her hair the best he could so Lorie could look normal for Autumn's college graduation and Zach's marriage to Kara Tomaszewski in May 2010.

After getting both our children moved to new locations as they began their adult lives, Lorie's July 2010 scans showed two more tumors. CyberKnife® again, this time with a new way of inserting the fiducials called SuperDimension Broncoscopy or SuperD for short, and a new kind of platinum fiducial that could not be coughed up as easily. The first week on the market Dr. Quinn tried one of each. The platinum fiducial stayed. The gold one did not so

CyberKnife® was delayed while the procedure was repeated. With no collapsed lung complicating matters, CyberKnife® was completed more quickly. On the eve of the final treatment, however, Lorie discovered a lump on her back while getting ready for bed. Dr. Wingate Clapper, her Radiation Oncologist, examined it before her last treatment and quickly scheduled her to see Dr. Hart again. Surgery within the week revealed the largest tumor Lorie has had to date, a tumor not even visible on a scan three weeks earlier. Scary stuff. *Scar*-y stuff too!

In these twelve years, Lorie lost over half her lung capacity. Nearly half of every year has been given to intensive treatments of one form or another, tethering us between our home, the clinic or the hospital. These limitations did not stop Lorie from living a full life though. She lived to see her children baptized, and her niece, and her sister, and her brother-in-law. She saw her children through high school, into college and even college graduation. She witnessed the marriage of our son. We now have the opportunity to walk alongside our daughter as she begins her profession, and to be present for our son and daughter-in-law's entrance into pastoral ministry.

Not long ago, it occurred to us that this cancer journey is not a chapter in our lives that will end and let us go on to other things. It is the whole book. There is no rescue. Not in this life, anyway. Nothing else will define us as much as how we managed a serious, long-term disease. So, rather than see this set of experiences as a handicap, we deliberately choose to see them as equipping us to be responsive to others. As a result, even when she did not feel well, Lorie has spoken at a number of public events, sharing how profoundly helpful her faith has been along the way. She has offered prayer and counsel to others struggling with persistent or terminal disease, especially a number who did not have strong family or church support systems as we have known. When asked how she holds it together, Lorie is fond of saying, "It is simple. I fight disease, not death."

Our next chapter unpacks the power of that statement.

CHAPTER TWO

Our approach: Fighting disease, not death

One of Mark's former students at the Christian Leadership Alliance's Steward Leaders Summit once posted a Facebook comment commending Mark as an example of perseverance in the middle of a spouse's suffering. The author was experiencing a number of overlapping circumstances. His wife had undergone major surgery in the middle of a job change and relocation of their family. His father was also severely injured in a fall. He felt Mark's example of pressing on in the middle of it all was a model he too would follow.

While this is kind, it is hardly deserved. It takes a lot of energy to remain focused on one's primary commitments when struggle has you in its grasp. The result of caring for a loved one with a long term illness has been compared to battle fatigue. And what about the person forced to bed for months at a time? Lorie's body is extensively marked with surgical scars. Her lungs wheeze. Walking up staircases leaves her winded. She has tattoos, not because she wanted to decorate her body in some way, but because they were needed to help radiation touch a precise spot. One doesn't have to be around her long to hear her cough when her frequent laughter requires more air than her lungs can provide. And that's just the damage that is visible!

Perseverance demands a whole life commitment. There isn't time to try to be a model for others, or to try to remain private so that one's family is not on public display. We can only focus on living. Today.

Lorie became a follower of Jesus at age eleven, during a time her parents experienced a spiritual renewal themselves. It coincided with her catechism and it made the instruction come alive. She began her Christian life hungry to learn all she could and she read extensively. She hung around the bible studies and prayer groups where her parents participated so she could learn more.

During her high school years, Lorie joined a Campus Life group and an ecumenical youth group her cousins attended. These good experiences fueled her hunger to serve others and she began holding bible studies in her parents' home that drew both youth and adults. She gained significant ministry experience even before she left for college.

Mark embraced Christ early in life. He grew up in a family that expected him to participate actively in church and school and to make a contribution as he did so. Acting honorably, completing one's tasks, and thinking critically are lessons his upbringing did not allow him to escape.

Both of us can point to mentors beyond our parents who took an interest in us, listened to us, and gave us guidance. Even more, they helped us avoid critical mistakes so many young adults make. None of these mentors were required to befriend us. They did it because of the type of people they were, and it strengthened our resolve to be like them as we had opportunity. We think these experiences prepared us to face lifelong struggle.

We met in college. Lorie was studying Christian Education, which she later put to use as the Minister of Youth and Young Adults for Indiana-Michigan Mennonite Conference for a number of years. Mark took a degree in biblical studies uncertain where it would ultimately lead him. We met because two of our good friends began dating during our freshman year and they invited us along. We also had an English class together where we were paired for a team assignment. Lorie later confessed she engineered the partnership because she thought teaming with Mark might help her get a better grade.

At the beginning of our sophomore year, Lorie was responsible for some incoming frosh events on behalf of the student government. Mark was also on campus early because he played on the soccer team. She invited him to help her move some tables and pick up supplies after his practice. This began a series of conversations that neither of us wanted to break off.

In spite of all the together time, Lorie turned Mark down flat when he first asked her out, telling him she already had a spouse picked out and there was no way she was marrying someone who did not hold a commitment to vocational ministry. Mark backed off. Days later, Lorie thought better of it and asked if

Mark remained interested. Mark felt that he didn't want to be number two on Lorie's list, and would just rather be friends.

The two of us kept seeking each other out at every opportunity to talk and walk. Our friends could see the romance developing even if we could not. It did not take long though. In the middle of our good friendship we found love. Once we admitted it to ourselves and each other, we could not think of ourselves as living without the other. We married on Mother's Day 1984.

During our engagement, Mark was invited to serve as a youth pastor for First Mennonite Church in Fort Wayne, Indiana. He became the senior pastor there shortly after we were married and we served the congregation until 1992. Both our children were born during this time.

First Mennonite was a congregation of one hundred members—a mix of Laotian and Chilean refugee families, persons of Appalachian descent and Swiss-German Mennonites. Located in an urban and neglected pocket of the city, the congregation had served as the original Fort Wayne Rescue Mission before the congregation spun it off during the Great Depression. The congregation was inter-generational and covered a wide range of economic strata.

During our years at First Mennonite we were given an extensive education in the problems humans face. Mark spent more time doing pastoral care in the court system than he ever did in the hospital. Every year brought tragic funerals and homes that ripped apart in contrast to the stable homes provided by our childhoods. The most painful experience of all was the loss of one of our newest and youngest fathers in our congregation—he and his unborn son. His wife and two other children were also seriously injured, all victims to the reckless driving of a young adult who decided to pass on a blind hill. Yet, through it all—the congregational members who were the products of or victims of incest, the senior citizens who had good reason to believe they might be attacked in their homes, the persons of international descent who walked through killing fields and survived refugee camps, the spouses trapped in unholy and violent relationships, the addictions and mental illnesses, the unwed mothers, and the children left to fend for themselves on the streets—there was a continuing triumph when the power of the gospel connected with the greatness of the human spirit. We met so many people who toughed it out and made something of themselves and their families, with good reason to sing praise to God and to serve others. We saw so much joy in the middle of the tragic that we think it found its way into our DNA somehow, preparing us to face our own trials.

By 1992, Mark had spent nine years at the church and finished his Master's degree. We had a growing feeling the congregation needed a pastor with a different set of gifts than Mark could bring, and we were in a position to leave on the best of terms. We also felt it would be a sign of good faith with the congregation if Mark resigned before he had any prospects for a new assignment. It became a wonderful experience to invite the elders of First Mennonite to help us pray and discern where we should ultimately go.

An offer finally came to be the candidate for a congregation near Chicago. By that time we had sold our home and moved everything into storage. The congregation that asked Mark to candidate was congregational in its governance, which means the congregation votes on whether to call a specific candidate to be their pastor. The process of getting to know the congregation was hostile from the beginning. The first question and nearly every question that followed in public question and answer times seethed with anxiety, anger and rejection that we did not immediately understand, especially because the accusations had no basis. To make matters worse, those who spoke in support of Mark seemed to share the same misperceptions.

It quickly became clear that the previous pastors (a husband and wife team) had been effective in helping people keep a set of issues at bay that erupted after their retirement, Mark serving as the focal point for the congregation's anxiety. It would not have mattered who the candidate was. People were using the opportunity to lash out. The system was disturbed enough that there would be attempts to sabotage nearly any candidacy as a way of acting out unassuaged grief.

This failed candidating experience was particularly hard on Lorie. She had dreams for years where she told off some of the key players for the way they mistreated her husband. Mark felt an unusual calm through it all, although he was finally able to name how it made him feel some time afterward. When he could finally say *shamed*, he had a good measure of healing.

As the mean-spiritedness of the candidating process began to peak and it became clear to Mark and then to others that the congregation would not affirm him, we discussed whether to withdraw. We both felt we should stay the course. God had called us to interact with this congregation, had he not? It didn't mean the congregation would agree or that it would ultimately extend a call. We should do whatever we could, however long we could, to be ministers of the gospel and offer salve for their hurt. They might not call us, but we could function as called people. They might not request our help, but we could be helpful in whatever window of opportunity we were given. At the least, we could hold our heads up and maintain our dignity, even if others felt they should try to strip it away. No matter the outcome, we should live as we believed that our faith made a difference. We would trust God and do our best to be gracious and kind.

A vote was finally taken, with the requirement that 75% of the congregation needed to affirm Mark as their pastor. Only 66% said yes.

We were suddenly unemployed, homeless and without prospects. Lorie's parents agreed to let us move in with them in Wisconsin until we could find work. Blessedly, within twenty-four hours of Mark contacting the Mennonite Church to re-establish his name on the list of pastors available to serve a congregation, we were contacted by the Indiana-Michigan Mennonite Conference. Were we interested in a position at the conference level? We wanted to make sure what was meant by "we." In the end it became a time and a half position that we split between us. It combined youth ministry resourcing for the hundred plus congregations of the Conference while directing programs at Amigo Centre, a newly expanded camp and conference center in Southern Michigan.

It took two months for the details to be worked out and for the conference to affirm us, and we nearly ran out of money, but it was a wonderful fit for our respective gifts and provided Lorie a professional outlet for her skills, skills honored through her subsequent ordination to ministry. We were so grateful for the support of both sets of parents, numerous friends and many colleagues during our first and brief period in Wisconsin. We were especially grateful for the kindness and encouragement of Rev. Ed and Margaret Homer and Rev. Anne Stuckey. They helped us hope that there would be a place where our ministry gifts would be welcome again. In fact, by God's grace, there came a time when Mark was able to talk with key members of the congregation that rejected him. Apologies and forgiveness traded places.

Our years with the Indiana-Michigan Mennonite Conference and Amigo Centre passed quickly, giving us broad exposure to a variety of congregations and putting us in touch with many more people who functioned joyfully in the face of overwhelming problems. Mark was particularly moved by one of his colleagues who had been abused and repeatedly rejected by her family, yet who warmly cared for her parents, served joyfully in her work, and cared deeply for her fellow employees.

We had agreed to work in this shared position for three years. Amigo Centre's programming gained such momentum that it became a full-time role after just one year. At the end of the three year term Lorie decided to continue in the youth ministry role, but Mark received an unexpected offer to direct *The Giving Project*, a five year stewardship education effort among North American Mennonite denominations. The project was to be based at Associated Mennonite Biblical Seminary in Elkhart, Indiana, a few miles from Lorie's office in Goshen. She would no longer have a forty mile commute from Sturgis, Michigan. Mark's office would be just around the corner from our children's schools. So, in the summer of 1995, we moved to Elkhart to begin a new stage of family life and ministry.

It was about this time that Lorie's health began to decline. It began as it does for so many women—heavy menstrual bleeding and longer periods. Lorie has always required a full night's sleep, but her need increased noticeably. Some days required a supreme effort to get out of bed. Over time Lorie began to show signs of anemia. We decided to have this looked at medically and it was determined Lorie had fibroids, irritating benign tumors many women experience and may live with their whole lives.

Lorie continued to bleed heavily and struggle with unrelenting fatigue over the next year. Aware that neither living with a diseased uterus nor having it removed via an early hysterectomy was desirable, she knew she needed to make a decision one way or another.

Two events the next year helped Lorie decide to have a hysterectomy. The first was a conversation with a nurse practitioner who encouraged her to be good to herself, take out the troubling tissue, suffer the inconvenience now, and then enjoy her children's years in our home to the fullest. The second was an opportunity to pray prayers for healing at our home congregation in Elkhart. Lorie has long pointed to this moment as the time she received real healing and complete peace. She needed to stop long enough to reorganize her life priorities by taking care of herself first. Then she could continue to care for her family and serve the Lord for the long haul. She points to this time as a healing of her resolve to live a life focused on God's direction in her life wherever that would lead. She did not know how much she would need the peace she experienced at the altar when a few months later the surgeon came into Lorie's room with those memorable words *You don't have cancer anymore!* God knew such a resolve needed to be firmly in place prior to any cancer diagnosis.

In the frightening weeks that followed we became grateful for a number of gifts given to us throughout our lives.

Gifts Given

First are the examples of our mentors and people with whom we had known community. Because of them we knew what perseverance looked like and that a person can survive the most horrid of circumstances.

Second on the list are our families of origin. Each of Lorie's grandmothers lived life fully in the middle of significant health issues. One was a sixty year survivor of colon cancer when all her siblings had succumbed to the disease. The other had cared for

Lorie's grandfather as he lived with disabling emphysema from too much time in grain silos. She was later diagnosed with a brain aneurysm, but it did not stop her from whitewater rafting, fishing trips or traveling to the homes of her grandchildren so she could care for the great-grandbabies as they were born. She experienced all this after surviving a South Dakota tornado at the age of thirteen. It snatched her from the fields and deposited her at another farm several miles away—scratched up, but alive. Lorie continues to look to these examples as she faces her difficult prognosis.

The many stories from both sides of Mark's family include that of a grandpa who was abandoned by his parents and who, along with Mark's longsuffering and faith-filled grandma, built an extensive farm in Northern Indiana during the Great Depression while teaching Sunday School and planting churches for more than forty years. He also had a grandmother who died from cancer when her five daughters were just beginning their families, and whose testimony of faith in the face of death is remembered still. Our privilege to have loving relationships with these people who had not shirked or shrank at the sight of their difficulties provided needed equipment for us to face ours.

A third gift we identify is money. While a ministry career is not a way to acquire a significant estate, Mark's father is a financial planner who advised us well from the time we were engaged. We also practiced the stewardship understandings Mark has written about and taught so extensively. A cancer diagnosis, as with any major disease, has a way of messing with family finances. In our case it included medical bills, loss of a spouse's income and concern about what future income would even look like, especially if and when the cancer returned, or worse, if it took Lorie's life. We were glad our savings financed the time it took to arrive at and adjust to a new normal, rather than going deeper into debt.

The greatest gift we believe we were given is our faith and what we learn from it. A skill we were taught in our college education was biblical reflection. It is a way of looking at life scenarios or moral choices, asking *"do the Scriptures speak to this in any way?"* If so, one spends time with those texts, noting principles to carry with them as they face the situation. We began and have continued this exercise of reflection throughout these years of battling cancer. It has proven to be the greatest source of strength for us, and it is because of this reflection that we came to understand we could fight disease with everything we have while not being anxious about death.

Here are a few texts we found especially meaningful:

Be anxious for nothing (Philippians 4:6-7)

In *The Muse*, the blog Mark maintains, he once wrote the following:

> *"Family members sometimes tease me as the person who never gets riled. I don't think that <u>never</u> is accurate, because when anger comes out of me it is not a pretty sight. I'm glad I have an understanding wife who has seen the rare sight*

more than others. I do celebrate the low blood pressure and general calmness I feel, however. I know that not carrying anxiety is far better than living with it. Interestingly, the more reasons I have had to be an anxious person in the middle of a battle for my wife's health, and the more opportunity I have taken to claim and live my faith, the more calm and nonplussed I have become. It has bred several results:

- *I don't stress about whether you are more theologically right or wrong in your views.*
- *Your desire to be faithful in service to others has become more important in how I assess a potential kindred spirit.*
- *Winning doesn't matter. Survival does. If I survive intact today, it is reason enough to celebrate.*
- *Ambition has disappeared. While I remain driven to work hard, preach with passion and keep developing knowledge that leads to wisdom, it doesn't have to be from the top of an organizational mountain.*

I'm finding a lot of scripture that confirms this understanding. I wish I had claimed their promises much, much earlier. Here is one I consider especially significant. 'Be anxious for nothing, but in everything by prayer and supplication with thanksgiving let your requests be made known to God. And the peace of God, which surpasses all comprehension, shall guard your hearts and your minds in Christ Jesus.' (Philippians 4:6, 7)

Rightly or wrongly, we have continued on because we enjoy life together, but even more because we believe that others will live longer and less expensively because we have embraced our ordeal as part of our participation in God's redemption of the world. Rightly or wrongly, we fight disease but not death—already content that God has not and is not ignoring us.

In this blog entry, Mark notes that not being anxious and relying on the peace of God helps us fight disease without needing to fight death. The moment of death is out of our control so there is no point being anxious about it. What is in our control is to live in such a way that we resist that which brings death, so that others may live full lives. This fills life with purpose rather than anxiety.

Our decisions to try radical or inventive treatment, even when the prognosis looked pretty bleak, are rooted in our determination to not be anxious and commitment to serve the well-being of others. There will be a time when a decision to continue treatment would only be an attempt to delay death. The benefit would then be negligible and would not increase knowledge or be of service to others. We hope to be just as non-anxious in that moment as we have striven to be thus far.

Living for future generations (Psalm 22)

One of the hardest moments we faced came during Lorie's MAID protocol, in the third year of battling cancer. It was seven months of prolonged hospitalization and being shut up in our home the remainder of the time. Her immunities were blown, so was her short-term memory. Mark refers to it as the darkest period for him, struggling not only with the loss of Lorie's vitality, but also her intellectual companionship. He simply wasn't prepared for the idea of Lorie continuing to live but not being emotionally present.

During this time our then twelve year old son Zach kept pressuring Mark to agree to re-marry should Lorie not survive the protocol. Zach could not imagine life without a mother. Our daughter, Autumn, could not have disagreed more. In her view there could never be a replacement. The pressure was nearly unbearable for Mark.

A key conversation with Nancy Snell, a former staffer for the Evangelical Lutheran Church of America, helped Mark greatly at this critical time. She had asked Mark how it was going and did so in such a way that she was waiting for more than a perfunctory answer. Mark told her about the pressures that weighed on him. He also mentioned how difficult it was to give Zach any kind of an answer because he knew how good our marriage had been, and how it set a seemingly impossible standard for any future marriage possibility.

In a gracious and loving way, yet with a needed directness, Nancy was able to tell Mark to grow up and think differently. "I have a marriage like you have," she said, "and what you need to do is stop mourning about the possibility of losing your marriage and thank God you have known such a gift. So many will go through their lifetimes, experiencing multiple marriages, and never know the kind of companionship and intimacy you and Lorie have known."

This was a wakeup call for Mark. Shortly afterward, he was reading Psalm 22 and came across this passage:

"Here's the story I'll tell my friends when they come to worship, and punctuate it with Hallelujahs: Shout Hallelujah, you God-worshipers; give glory, you sons of Jacob; adore him, you daughters of Israel. He has never let you down, never looked the other way when you were being kicked around. He has never wandered off to do his own thing; he has been right there, listening.

Here in this great gathering for worship I have discovered this praise-life. And I'll do what I promised right here in front of the God-worshipers. Down-and-outers sit at God's table and eat their fill. Everyone on the hunt for God is here, praising him. 'Live it up, from head to toe. Don't ever quit!'

From the four corners of the earth people are coming to their senses, are running back to God. Long-lost families are falling on their faces before him. God has taken charge; from now on he has the last word.

All the power-mongers are before him—worshiping! All the poor and powerless, too—worshiping! Along with those who never got it together—worshiping!

Our children and their children will get in on this. As the word is passed along from parent to child. Babies not yet conceived will hear the good news — that God does what he says."

This Psalm is written by one who is suffering an excruciating and debilitating existence. Christians often consider earlier verses in this Psalm a look ahead to the sufferings of the Messiah because there are uncannily accurate descriptions of aspects of a crucifixion. One can also choose to read it from the perspective of AIDS, Lou Gehrig's disease, cancer or some other excruciating illness. The words Mark read are the conclusion reached by the suffering person who wrote the Psalm; they would continue to look to God and proclaim God's faithfulness. They might not be able to see why God was faithful at the moment, but looking back over the history of God's people and the course of their lives, they could. And anticipating the future, they would do their part to proclaim this faithfulness to children not yet born.

Mark couldn't wait to get to the hospital bed, and even though he knew Lorie would not recall when he first read her these verses, this passage became a reference point for each new diagnosis. We will stand and proclaim the faithfulness of God to anyone who will listen for as long as we are able. We will serve those who come after us. We will extend as much love as we can to our children and our children's children and your children's children. This is the highest purpose of our lives and we keep pledging ourselves to it.

Praying for trifles (2 Kings 3)

Another scripture passage gripped Mark during this time—a narrative from the Hebrew scripture that rarely gets told.

The scene is 2 Kings 3, when the northern tribes of Israel are at war with Moab. King Ahab of Israel had died and the King of Moab decided to not pay his annual tribute of sheep any longer. The kings of Israel, Judah and Edom assembled in an alliance against Moab and set out for battle. They got lost in the wilderness, however, and troops and animals began to languish from extreme thirst.

Elisha the prophet was summoned to see if he could ask God for guidance and rescue. The story shows Elisha to be a bit grouchy at the prospect, but he eventually agrees. Then he utters a most remarkable phrase: *"This is only a trifle in the sight of the Lord. . . ."* (2 Kings 3:18 NRSV).

Elisha goes on to say that God would provide water in the desert without there being any rain or wind. The story concludes with water flowing out of Edom and filling the desert the next morning.

Mark got enamored with the word *trifle*, which means a very small thing. Trifle echoes with other words like *glance* or *pittance* or *vestige*—something small and barely registering. In other words, the barest nod from God could slake the thirst of three combined armies.

The notion of a trifle began to affect our prayers—especially in moments when the anguish felt insurmountable. A trifle for God is an outstanding miracle for us. A trifle for God is an answer to our prayers that we could not possibly imagine and as a result would not have asked for.

Our prayers went something like this:

God, send us a trifle.
or
*God, glance our way and notice us
if even just for a moment.*
or
*God, we would gladly accept one of your
throw away efforts.*

Praying in this way put us in a mental frame where we accepted that our circumstances were beyond our power, and that the way we would prefer to live might not be possible any longer. Still, we would accept God's faithful action on our behalf, rejoicing in what it would bring, believing that it would be even better than what we could construct on our own in full health. This mental frame strengthens us to fight what we can fight—disease and dis-ease—while living within our limitations, namely that we are finite and mortal.

By His stripes we are healed (Isaiah 53:5)

A scripture that has been of significant help for Lorie comes from the prophet Isaiah, another passage many Christians believe points to the sufferings of Jesus.

> *"But He was wounded for our transgressions,*
> *He was bruised for our iniquities;*
> *The chastisement for our peace was upon Him,*
> *And by His stripes we are healed."*
> *(Isaiah 53:5 NKJV)*

The phrase *by his stripes we are healed* reminds Lorie that her ultimate healing is already won in the sufferings of Jesus, and like him, she does not have to resist death. Instead, she can live her years, however short they may be, in the same spirit. She can let her trauma and resulting scars be a living witness that she fought disease and helped bring life to others.

It is for God's glory (John 9:3)

Lorie is occasionally asked to preach in a church or speak to a group about her faith and approach to suffering. She has often needed to back out due to yet another cancer diagnosis that compromises her immunities and makes her housebound again. When she has been able, however, she often refers to the story of the man born blind—a story found in the 9th chapter of John's gospel.

She finds that in nearly every audience there is a group of people who think illness or suffering is a sign that God is displeased and that God's judgment is somehow the source of the illness. There is also a group of persons who think it is presumptuous or selfish to ask God for miracles. Maybe you do not know anyone who holds to either point of view, but we can assure you such people are legion and they make life difficult for the suffering person. One group tells the sufferer they need to confess their sins if they ever want to be made whole again. The other berates the suffering person for being selfish and asking big things of God. Making use of the John 9 text, Lorie points to the words of Jesus as a means to move beyond these tired and silly perspectives and invites her audiences to see matters differently.

These diverse religious perspectives were characteristic of how people thought in Jesus' day too. The followers of Jesus thought sin—either by the blind man or his parents—was the reason he had been struck blind. After Jesus healed him, the Pharisees took Jesus to task for violating what was proper and performing a miracle on a Sabbath day. Because he did so, they viewed Jesus as the sinner in the story and certainly not a servant of God.

The verse that guides Lorie's own responses to suffering are these words of Jesus:

"Neither this man nor his parents sinned . . . but this happened so that the work of God might be displayed in his life." (John 9:3 NIV)

Lorie inserts her own diagnosis into these words and invites the suffering person and their families to do so as well.

"My leiomyosarcoma did not happen because I or my parents sinned . . . this happened so that the work of God might be displayed in my life."

Perhaps this sounds ridiculous. To some ears it might even sound as if the person who speaks it credits God for inflicting them with something. Consider it a statement of faith and hope, however, a belief there is some purpose and benefit rather than none at all. Understood that way, it is far less ridiculous and perhaps more sane than giving up, ranting at the heavens, or believing that nothing more can be done.

From our own circumstances we know this to be true. Lorie is now believed to be the longest lived person with the metastatic disease. Her experiences and course of treatment now benefit others who share her diagnosis. New patients are able to progress to more advanced medicines and surgical procedures and skip the more traumatic ones because Lorie bears the stripes in her body that truly are a means of healing for others. They are able to prolong their lives and perhaps outlive Lorie because she chose the orientation of letting the work of God be displayed in her life.

Yet another powerful example

Perhaps the best way to conclude our description of how we approach lifelong suffering is to share an example from another family.

Mark is privileged to serve as the Acting President of the Christian Leadership Alliance. One of his fellow board members is a man named Joe Krivickas, a widower and father of young children. His wife Lisa was a physician who passed on to glory after a brutal battle with Lou Gehrig's disease. With Joe's permission, we want to share an excerpt they sent to friends and prayer supporters during Lisa's last weeks of life.

July 17, 2009 - <u>Staying the Course</u>

After 10 days in the Neuro Trauma ICU and 8 days in Spaulding Rehabilitation Hospital, Lisa came home. . .in a much weaker state than when she left . . . .On June 26th Lisa had a "minor" surgical procedure to implant a pump that will deliver an experimental medication directly into Lisa's spinal fluid. There were complications and Lisa had to travel a rough road the past 20 days . . . . Now, after spending four nights at home, Lisa has bravely decided to go back to the hospital for three days and two nights so that the implanted pump can be activated and the treatment [can] be started. On Wednesday, Lisa courageously said, "If I went through this much pain I might as well finish the course and complete the treatment. . . ."

As you may recall, we wrote . . . that Lisa agreed to be the first subject of a risky medical trial that has not been used on humans. The treatment is at the cellular level. The pump they put inside Lisa will inject a medication directly into Lisa's spinal fluid and, at the cellular level, attempt to shut down each cell from manufacturing the "bad" proteins that cause ALS. The trial is risky, but it could provide extremely valuable information on the safety and tolerability of this treatment approach for ALS and other similar disorders. Lisa's love for her family and friends, along with her desire to help others, is motivating her to "stay the course." Lisa believes that she should do whatever she can to potentially prolong her life and help others. It is written in Chapter 5 of the book of Romans: ". . . because we know that suffering produces perseverance; perseverance, character; and character, hope. And hope does not disappoint us."

In Lisa, unfortunately, we have seen her "suffering." We also have seen the strength of her "perseverance" and "character." And, in some way that only God is aware of, all those who Lisa touches are able to see a "hope" that will "not disappoint us."

—Lisa, Joe, Brooke and Chase Krivickas

A-men and A-men.

Lorie and Mark in August 2001. Lorie was barely recovered from her first lung resection and had already learned the cancer was back.

Lorie with our children in June 2002, during the sixth round of the MAID protocol. At this point she barely remembered our visits.

Lorie at Loch Ness, Easter week 2003. The time between her third and fourth occurrences of cancer gave our family time for a rare vacation. We took full advantage of it.

Relay for Life June 2003. Dr. Paul LeMarbe, Lorie's brother David Sonnentag and cousins Linda Apple and Sarah Meyer join the laughter that always surrounds Lorie. Sarah was the flower girl at our wedding.

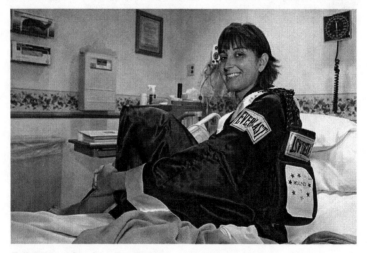

Fall 2005. After Lorie's third lung resection and surviving her seventh round of cancer, Mark gave Lorie her very own boxing robe and gloves.

Relay for Life 2006. Lorie was in the middle of radiation for a C2-C3 tumor, using the bandana to keep her neck from sun exposure. She would soon have her fourth lung resection.

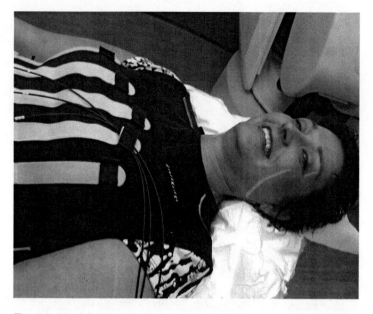

The advent of CyberKnife® technology felt like we were in a Science Fiction movie, but it sure beats lung resections!

Lorie in 2008. New chemotherapy helped us keep five tumors at bay, but Lorie's hair fell out again. Her stocking hat reads *Off-target Effect*, a reference to unintended, and in this case beneficial, medical results.

Our family in May 2009, with Lorie's hair growing back again. From left to right: Mark, Autumn, Lorie, Kara and Zach. Kara and Zach married in May 2010.

Lorie at our daughter's graudation and our son's wedding, May 2010. Eleven years and thirteen cancer occurrences were in the rear view mirror.

CHAPTER 3

Other Approaches:
Not fighting disease and not fighting death

In 1992, Frank Reynolds was hit from behind in a car accident that left him paralyzed from the waist down. Three years later—three years of not using his legs—he was inspired by the movie *Lorenzo's Oil* to change his therapy regimen with the hope of restoring some neural connections in his back. He succeeded: now capable of walking five miles a day and driving again, albeit it in constant pain.

Frank now runs a startup company devoted to improving the chances for others with spinal cord injury. This display of sheer will to make something good out of what one has been handed, is a fine example of fighting disease (injury in this case) while not fighting death. Our response to disease or injury we have control over, death we do not. And yes, it is worth noticing that fighting disease as hard as Frank does often has the benefit of delaying death. In our household we say it this way: *"Let's not die before we are dead!"* This is not the approach many people take, however. We hear from a good number who think one should give up, surrender, embrace or accept one's condition—in short, fight neither disease nor death.

Not fighting because of theology

A theology is essentially what someone believes about God. What one believes about God leads some to conclude that neither disease nor death is to be struggled against. They believe that whatever happens flows from divine intention and that this intention must be accepted if one is to bring honor to God. A person might be heard to say, *"I've resigned myself to my fate."* Or, they might encourage a suffering person to stop fighting the will of God.

When Lorie was at her worst, a number of loving people travelled to Wisconsin to visit us and say goodbye. They wanted to bring the chapter of their friendship with Lorie to a close since they were certain death was imminent. And indeed, Lorie was gravely ill. When she survived, though, it was difficult to re-engage these relationships because goodbyes had been said and Lorie had been grieved over. They had moved on. They found saying "hello again" more difficult than saying goodbye.

Over the years Lorie has been accused of faking it, of exaggerating the seriousness of her cancer, and even of bringing economic and emotional harm to her family by not succumbing to the disease. In all instances the assumption is that diagnosis is equal to death, and the dying person should let go and let God's (or Mother Nature's) intentions come to fruition. So, if Lorie has not died, she must not really be that sick.

As with all theological distortions, some measure of truth is present. Of course we do well to accept the existence of our suffering. We do even better, however, by embracing the promise of God's grace that we are not ultimately defined by the sin or disease that so easily harms us. If we are supposed to just accept what we mistakenly believe God has decreed, we would not wear glasses; remove unsightly hair growing from nostrils, ears or chins, nor repair club feet, cleft palates or crossed-eyes. The two of us often remind people with this erroneous understanding that Jesus said, *"Suffer the little children to come unto me,"* NOT *"Suffer, little children, and come unto me."*

Our daughter, Autumn, has some congenital mid-range hearing loss that often makes it difficult to understand what people are saying if there is ambient noise. If she believed she must resign herself to this deficit, she would never have learned to compensate by watching a speaker's lips or hand motions to confirm what she thinks they are saying. By fighting the deficit she has picked up a remarkable ability to persist to understand and confirm the details of her work assignments. It has also enhanced her ability to work with other unique learning styles among the children in her classroom.

Can you think of anyone admired for giving up in despair? We can't.

Not fighting because one enjoys the attention

Others refuse to fight because the attention they receive becomes a treasure they loathe to lose. Rather than resign themselves in stoic silence and withdrawal from the world they once knew, such a person enjoys each symptom as if it were something delicious. They savor the attention that comes with each visit, each medical test, each doctor's appointment, each new level of bad news that they will share with anyone who will listen. They believe that suffering in some way gives them permission to expect special treatment.

For some this may be because it is the first time they feel special, or because they derive their self-worth from how others treat them. They might say *"Don't bother about me."* But what they mean is *"Please DO make a fuss over me in my rapidly declining condition."*

Serving in ministry gives occasion to meet many such persons. Often they are shut-in and expect pastoral visits, during which time they recite the litany of no one cares or visits, how the doctors aren't listening, and how the church never reaches out. The irony of this miserable-ing is that our visit was, in fact, an act of reaching out from the church. While we are there a grandchild calls, a neighbor stops by to see if they can pick up any groceries because they are on the way to the store, and we learn that the children are busily planning a lavish 85th birthday celebration. Too often shut-ins choose to shut themselves in.

One of the most egregious examples Mark witnessed was at the Boston airport. A frail, wheel-chair bound elderly woman suddenly discovered she could leap, walk and run in order to beat him to the one remaining luggage cart. Then she collapsed back into her wheel-chair for her companion to push her.

Many people are frail and need assistance. But some do choose to milk it—ultimately dying before they are dead.

Not fighting the process

We also encountered some who view disease and death as a linear process—a staged event one must progress through in exact ways. As arm-chair scholars, they look up Lorie's disease to read about how it presents itself and progresses, or they read about the stages of grief and believe everyone passes through all the stages in the same way—forgetting that typical case studies or clinical descriptions are generalizations and nothing more.

A pastor once came to confront Lorie, convinced Lorie was stuck in the denial stage of her dying process. Unless Lorie could admit she was truly dying, this pastor believed, then Lorie could never deal with her anger over the diagnosis. Not dealing with her anger meant Lorie would die without coming to peace with her shortened life. Lorie's protests that she had already lived through her denial, and ultimately arrived at a measure of peace to face whatever might come, was viewed as a false piousness, continued denial, and a refusal to accept the pastoral counsel Lorie was being offered. The pastor left in frustration.

While we agree that learning about disease and death equips one to recognize what is happening and to make plans as the progression unveils itself, one should be aware that outliers lie everywhere. For instance, Lorie has a rare form of a rare cancer, and has a rare reaction to certain medications, yet is one of the longest-lived survivors of this disease. NO case study or clinical observation could predict her journey with disease, even if they were able to help with diagnosis and a theory about how to treat it.

Similarly, no two persons will have the same journey through their lifetimes. Each of us is a rare collection of outlying experiences far removed from the average description, even though there are patterns we can recognize in everyone's life.

We think these outliers are the reasons to fight disease. Outliers are the places discoveries are made that eventually become the new average that can benefit others. By fighting disease and not just succumbing to the next stage, suffering of persons in the future gets lessened.

Not fighting as a matter of justice

Then there is the argument of economic justice:

> *"How can you devote so much money to yourself, trying to extend your life, when your children might be deprived of a college education?"*
>
> -asked by a friend

> *"If I were terminal, I'd want to avoid heroic measures and use the money to inoculate children from disease."*
>
> -said to Lorie at a dinner party by a church official

"When is your insurance company going to start denying your claims so there is money for the rest of us?"
-a tech, when Lorie's lung collapsed, requiring further surgical intervention

"Haven't you done enough?"
-a nurse

"Call hospice and see what services they will provide. Further surgery isn't warranted and chemotherapy or radiation won't help."
-Lorie's first oncologist in Indiana, 2001.

"Over and above reasonable and customary. . . .
Over and above reasonable and customary . . . .
Over and above reasonable and customary . . . ."
-our former health insurance company, on every bill once we had a cancer diagnosis.

Lorie is allergic to narcotics. We wish that for every dose of morphine she did not receive an equivalent number of dollars was donated to a medical mission, but the economics of medicine do not work that way, and does not even in socialized medicine.

Medical discovery is expensive. Further, many discoveries are unintended effects of research set up for other purposes—hence the power of outliers. By devoting money and resources to research (and hopefully without over-regulating or over-litigating the discovery process) we are able to make medical discoveries that continue to make more effective treatments common and affordable. Penicillin and small pox vaccines are two high profile examples. In Lorie's case, multiple CyberKnife® treatments even on multiple tumors have been demonstrated. This means future sufferers of leiomyosarcoma can be treated without hospital stays, months of surgical recovery, and perhaps without going on disability. Is this not a pursuit of justice? Is this not building a legacy out of what one was given? Is this not standing in the tradition of the One by whose stripes we can know the healing of our souls?

Judaism teaches the principle of tzedekah (righteousness/justice). In his book, *The Kabbalah of Money* Shambhala Press, 2001), Rabbi Nilton Bonder describes engaging in tzedekah as participation in the celestial economy. For example, by being a business person who charges a fair price, demonstrates excellent customer service as a matter of integrity, and carries out their affairs justly, that business person not only does a good business here on earth, they also store up assets of goodwill and grace in God's account—grace they might need to draw on in a time of crisis.

This is the type of justice we want to practice. We believe our commitment to it brought the benefit of being able to receive withdrawals when we needed them most.

Our experience leads us to mourn for those who do not have a community of family or friends such as ours. Perhaps they are victims of incredible cruelty, or perhaps it is a lifestyle choice that leaves them bereft at the inauguration of suffering. So many are abandoned unjustly at the time of their greatest need. So many are treated with prejudice or callousness so that physical illness becomes but one item on their long and continuing list of anguish.

Living with cancer is unimaginably hard. Every case is unique because of the person, their family system, and their unique set of choices and experiences that come with them. Everyone who faces it is in a unique territory no one else can fully perceive. How awful it must be to enter that territory with no traveling companions, multiplying and far-reaching concerns and the echo of rejection as loved ones walk away!

Jesus tells us that those of us who mourn will be comforted. Whether we mourn our disease or the disease of others and the additional suffering they inflict on us, this is a wonderful promise to know. What we must realize is that this comfort often happens at the hand of others, and that their ability to comfort us exists in proportion to our having lived an others-centered life from the beginning.

Not fighting: an existential perspective

One other way we have seen the failure to fight disease or death is through the existential denial of its existence. The person who receives the diagnosis is put out of mind by family and friends as if that person no longer exists. When someone says, *"I don't know what to say,"* or *"I didn't want to bother them,"* what they mean is, *"I don't want my reality to be bothered with this."*

Family and friends just up and disappear. Spouses walk out because this is not what *in sickness and health* meant for them. Even the person diagnosed with the disease may try to run pell-mell toward a life they feel is denied them, abandoning spouses and children in the process. On several occasions Mark has had clients cancel contracts on the eve of learning that Lorie had a new cancer occurrence. Others have threatened to cancel because they feel he will be too distracted to do his work well. We can tell you that the bigger distraction is the worry that income will be taken away!

Or consider the person with herpes that continues to knowingly infect multiple partners, pretending their diagnosis never happened. This too is existential denial.

Or how about the general obtuseness many of us choose in regard to the severe suffering of so many— whether through war, planned famine, enslavement, grinding poverty or preventable disease?

At the heart of all these denials of both disease and death lies a fear that we will not know how to cope if suffering and death are the reality instead of our pre-tend worlds of creature comfort and antiseptic living. Indeed, we argue that fear lies at the heart of all these approaches when someone expects others to choose to remain on the bed of paralysis instead of grinding through excruciating rehab in order to reclaim the power to walk, or to walk away from hope simply because the cost of treatment means a patient must sell their family home but the family refuses.

Max Lucado's little booklet *Living Without Fear* puts it as profoundly as any:

> *"Fear never wrote a symphony or poem, negotiated a peace treaty, or cured a disease. Fear never pulled a family out of poverty or a country out of bigotry. Fear never saved a marriage or a business. Courage did that. Faith did that. People who refused to consult or cower to their timidities did that. But fear itself. Fear herds us into a prison and slams the doors."*

We choose to shake off the manacles and live free!

CHAPTER 4

Other Approaches:
Fighting disease and fighting death

We are privileged to have worked with the renowned singer-composer Ken Medema on a variety of projects. As an example, Mark and Ken presented together on *The Offering as Worship* (Design Group International and Ken Medema Music, 2006) for multiple audiences across the country. Ken is blind from birth and builds on this limitation in a variety of ways that give him sight beyond what sighted people can perceive.

Once, Mark picked Ken up at the Grand Rapids airport to take him to the home of his assistant and road manager, Bev VanderMolen. Mark mistakenly drove into a driveway just a couple of houses away from Bev's home. It looked like her home to Mark, but Ken immediately knew it was not because the angle of the driveway was slightly different. He could feel his location far more accurately than Mark could see it.

Ken's life is a witness about building one's life upon what one has and what one can control, rather than getting stuck on one's deprivation. Some take a different view, however. They remain stuck on the idea that physical limitations and physical sufferings are our responsibility. If we get sick, stay sick, or are faced with an overwhelming problem, someone caused it and it can be undone if only we try hard enough. The intended outcome is for the problem to disappear, not for it to be turned into an asset.

Just as some choose not to fight disease or death, some think both must be fought against. Those who fight both have a theological starting point too.

Word-Faith

It is not our intention to point fingers at anyone, so we are not going to trace the history or identify key leaders of the word-faith movement. Instead, we want to relate our experiences as they came to us.

A word-faith orientation believes that the words we speak need to agree with the words God declared—especially those written in Scripture. Our prayers must proclaim our faith, not our doubts, as that leaves room for the devil and his minions to wreak havoc in our lives. These words, in and of themselves, are believed to have power when they are uttered because they are God-breathed. They have the power to heal, to bless or to curse contained within them. This means one should not admit they have a disease because this grants power to the disease and makes it real in a reverse, perverse *Velveteen Rabbit* sort of fashion. The implications of this point of view are troubling:

- If one gets sick or remains sick it is because they sinned or do not believe.
- If someone dies before old age and natural causes take them, it is because they did not lay claim to God's promises. Wayward family members are singled out as the reason why someone dies. Pastors not able to pray a powerful enough healing prayer are accused of no longer having the anointing of the Holy Spirit on them.
- The onus for getting well becomes almost like wizardry—the words we speak, the prayers we pray, and the spiritual gifting of those who pray are used as if they were magical powers one summons against the dark forces of the devil.

We readily concede that the problems of sin and death are indeed problems. We also concede that disease and death can be acquired conditions because of our choices or the choices of others (see the next chapter), but in most cases the source is vestigial to our fallen world: the environment in which we were raised, a misplaced gene, a side effect of giving birth, being in the wrong place at the wrong time, or ingesting something tainted. So many causes of suffering are indirect and the damage is permanent regardless of one's positive attitude or spoken affirmations of faith in God. One's positive and hopeful outlook simply does not shape the diagnosis, no matter how much benefit it may prove to be during therapy, treatment, or while converting the problem into some form of asset.

When our son was twelve, Lorie was deathly ill. A woman accosted him after church one day, instructing him to pray for his mother every night or she would die. During the same period, a woman who was gracious enough to bring us a meal attempted to push past Lorie's mother and rush upstairs to our bedroom to lay hands on Lorie and pray, convinced that her prayer would bring healing. She was unconcerned with the fact the Lorie's immune system was severely compromised, or that she had just crawled back into bed and was asleep after an extended episode of retching.

We have been roused out of a sound sleep several times by people at all night prayer meetings, calling us to ask if a certain evangelist could pray, RIGHT NOW, and so that they all could claim that their prayers healed Lorie.

Then there are the specially anointed handkerchiefs, diet supplements made from biblical recipes and anointing oil brought back from the Mount of Olives. If only these prayers could be offered by the right person and combined with the materials and our faith, Lorie would be completely healed and live the full measure of her years. Any refusal to participate, or even a slightly cocked eyebrow of doubt on our part becomes an indictment of our lack of belief in God, our giving ourselves to the power of the devil, and perhaps a demonstration of generational sin that we have yet to confess.

It is disconcerting to have someone rebuke you because of the way you pray, to be told to listen to someone's CD or podcast on healing or else you will suffer the consequences, or to be told to be silent about any of your symptoms because speaking it makes it come true. But the bigger problem comes when a suffering person is in their last hours and then passes away.

- Instead of the suffering person or their family being comforted and allowed to grieve, they are told to try harder and made to feel guilty, or worse, to try to figure out whose sin brought about the death.
- Instead of being given relief from pain, the dying person is encouraged to forsake medication and show greater faith. Sometimes the pressure comes from spouses or children who can't bear to see their loved ones go, further complicating already strained family relationships and the ability for people to grieve in healthy ways.
- In many cases the dying person's affairs are not put in order because to do so is to admit one is dying. This further compounds reasons for grief and suffering among surviving family members who must wait for the end of the probate process before pensions or life insurance policies or bank accounts can be accessed.

Rather than the type of physical blindness that one overcomes, as has our friend Ken Medema, this is a blindness of faith that cripples the ability to live through one's suffering.

Extreme Measures

Not getting one's affairs in order is a common problem for those who try to fight both disease and death—especially for those who cannot bring themselves to admit they are terminal. In an attempt to cheat death, they end up cheating their loved ones from tender moments at the end, and from being able to move on with their lives after the suffering one dies.

Some of the stories we could point to have high profiles: the celebrity or billionaire that starts a new family when in their seventies, the wealthy eccentric that dies without a will, or even the person who tries to reach out from beyond the grave to control their family through the instructions in the Last Will and Testament they did write. More often than not, trying to cheat death occurs as one pursues the latest miracle cure or wacky theory devoid of all logic or analysis, or by trying every heroic measure to delay one's passing.

We recognize that these are personal and difficult decisions belonging to the individual and their families. We also recognize that suffering people often must make decisions without warning and without a clear indication of what the result will be. We certainly faced such a moment when we chose for Lorie to go through the MAID Protocol. There were many reasons not to! We maintain, however, that there is a difference between the agony of possibly making one's life even shorter in the treatment of a terminal condition, versus the agony that results from denying that one is terminal at all, or refusing to say good-bye, or do anything to stem the grief of loved ones.

We remember one friend who continued to maintain they would be healed and would go home in the hours just before their death, even after it was agreed no remaining measures existed. Their spouse was even stronger in this point of view. How could the family begin to plan a funeral or take care of their affairs or allow themselves to grieve?

These friends stood in contrast with the scene when Mark's Aunt Lois died of pancreatic cancer. Her last weeks were filled with happy visits from family and friends as Lois had strength to bear it. She was able to die as she had lived. Her sense of household—the large sprawling community of neighbors and family—simply shifted to her hospital room. She fought the disease hard but death was not an enemy.

Magical Thinking

We have already touched on the unrealistic expectations of those who think praying a certain way or drinking a certain tea will provide a cure, but magical thinking isn't just an aspect of a word-faith orientation or one's pursuit of extreme measures. Rather, it can be an approach to suffering all by itself. Magical thinking in this sense means that a person believes their efforts make all the difference.

It is magical thinking to believe that undoing or avenging what was done makes suffering go away. Ask a family member of a murdered loved one whether the execution of the murderer brings them a final resolution. Or ask a diabetic who finally gets their insulin levels improved whether it helped them re-grow the foot they lost to the disease.

It is magical thinking to believe that belief makes problems go away. Yes, belief equips a person to face problems more effectively than does feeling hopeless, but who among us can mentally will problems away just because we do not want to have any?

And it is definitely magical thinking to believe one should never or will never suffer. Only those completely seduced by the comforts and power of wealth could think such a thing is even possible. Yet, magical thinking continues to complicate the approach to suffering. Too many find their struggles deeper still, simply because they think it is all up to them to avoid them, deny them, or somehow move beyond them.

Why we don't fight death

Fighting disease might look like one is fighting death, but it is not. Certainly death might be delayed because of one's approach to suffering, but death is not an enemy any longer. At least, not from a Christian point of view.

The Christian believes victory over death has been won, that the mortal body will be transformed into something wholly renewed, as Christ was in his resurrection body, and that the life that really is life is the life to come. The Christian does not try to escape this life with all its ugly struggle, but assumes the attitude of Jesus Christ, who did not shrink from suffering but used his life as an instrument of healing, service and salvation for others.

We have little power over the where and when of our disease and ultimate demise. Nearly all of us are guaranteed that we will lie down for a time before we fall all the way down. And when we lie down it will be a bed of affliction for most of us. Such is the ultimately unavoidable human condition. Our power exists in the perspective we choose, our orientation toward others, and Who it is we choose to follow as our model in life...and death.

CHAPTER 5

Other Approaches:
Inviting disease and death

When our now adult children were merely a babe in arms and a toddler, Lorie and I were privileged to hear Joni Eareckson Tada speak at the old RCA Dome in Indianapolis. She was paralyzed in a diving accident as a teenager, but has used her chair as a platform to sing, paint, write, speak and host a radio program for many years. After many years in a wheelchair she now lives with chronic pain and has become a breast cancer survivor.

The place was packed and there were hundreds of people in the front rows that made the place look like a hospital ward. Wheel chairs, hospital beds and people with enormously visible disabilities were front and center. We wondered if this was what it was like for Jesus during his earthly ministry—people coming from everywhere with sick, crippled, palsied or possessed friends and family members, hoping for a word, a touch or a prayer that might bring healing.

The lights went down in the house and spotlights flooded the stage. The audience quieted as Joni was introduced and wheeled onto the stage. But somehow, in the process of transporting her to center stage, her catheter tube disconnected, the bag emptied, and her urine began pooling around her on the floor. She looked down and observed the problem, telling us what had happened. And then, in the middle of her gathering waste, and with the heads of all those suffering souls nodding their affirmations, she testified beautifully to the grace of God and the contentment she labored to find in her helplessness.

It remains such a profound memory for the two of us that it is difficult to refrain from weeping whenever we speak of it. That moment, as much as any other, reminds us of why we battle the human limitations we face while ceasing to worry about the, "*what* and *when* and *how much*" questions of life.

This is not the response some choose. In the preceding chapters we discussed our experiences and reflections regarding those who choose to give up and surrender to suffering and those who think both must be railed against. There remains one more approach to describe and critique: that of inviting disease and death, or worse, inflicting disease and death on others.

Inflicting in Ignorance

We wonder if some of you will dismiss the possibility of this inflictive response to suffering. If this is your reaction, we do not want to be guilty of judging your cynicism, but we must admit we believe your incredulity comes from having lived a sheltered life—often intentionally. Living in a wealthy culture makes it possible to create one's own version of paradise, and many of us have done it. When we get caught up in materialistic living it becomes easy to equate a bad haircut as time in purgatory, or not scoring tickets for the opening night of a blockbuster movie as an evening spent in hell. When one's only experience with disease and death is from a distance—viewed in sound bites or as forms of entertainment—it can be difficult to understand that evil provides a very real presence, and that evil is as near at hand as God is promised to be.

Worse, such a person may manufacture their own suffering and thereby make others suffer, in part because they choose not to learn from the experiences of others. Addictions, failed families and tragic deaths often accompany celebrity lifestyles, serving as prominent examples of other persons living by the same ignorance. We could learn from them and thereby avoid the same mistakes, but not if we keep choosing the same insulated ignorance.

Even more subtle is a preening arrogance that sniffs at lower standards of living left behind as a person becomes wealthy, and that now makes unrealistic demands of people who serve at restaurants, hotels and shopping centers.

"I can't possibly buy this house! The surface of the workroom countertop is so low rent!"

"Waiter, I've spilled soup on my fly! You WILL cover my dry cleaning bill won't you?"

"My team played so badly, and I'm so mad that I spent so much on the tickets that I'm going to yell at the first person who tells me to have a nice day!"

"I am astonished that you used the word 'yes' instead of 'affirm' in the draft of the proposal and suggest you be formally reprimanded!"

"Nurse! I don't care if there is a code blue next door. I've already asked twice for more ice chips!"

This drip, drip, drip of unreasonable and impossible expectation borne from stilted capacity for empathy leaves many wounded and newly angry persons in one's wake. All too often, the person doing the inflicting does not care who they harm, even if it is pointed out.

Lashing Out

Some responses to suffering might seem mild or excusable and often happen as the initial response to tragic news, a devastating diagnosis, or in the wake of a natural disaster. By mild, we mean that allowing oneself to indulge in lashing out is not characteristic of the person. They experience embarrassment or even deep remorse after they catch their breath and have a moment to reflect. Still, throwing things, yelling at the doctor, looting a store knocked open by an earthquake, having a quickie affair because disease is not what was bargained for: these are often flash and uncharacteristic expressions chosen in the moment, causing new layers of suffering for those suffering already, and adding new victims along the way.

Lorie was once accosted by a woman who had been diagnosed with advanced cancer and was struggling to make sense of the news. They were both in the radiation dressing room after having finished that day's treatment. The woman grabbed Lorie by the shoulders and shook her.

"How can you be so happy?" she railed, blustering on about how unfair it all was and how she could not cope. Lorie's joyful spirit—never having met the woman—was an insult added on top of this woman's injured spirit and diseased body. As she shook Lorie, she clearly had not considered Lorie's physical weakness from so much treatment, or her susceptibility to infection because of significantly reduced immunity. This woman was so embroiled in her own anger that she was unaware of her effect on others in her moment of lashing out.

Some friends of ours saw their family life crumble into dust when cancer was diagnosed. The spouse with the diagnosis acted upon the errant belief that they would be denied certain joys they now earnestly desired to seize. Normally, seizing the day sounds like a good approach, but not when it means starting an affair, nearly bankrupting the rest of the household, cutting off relationships with one's children, embarrassing one's aging parents, and depriving loved ones of the opportunity to be present and supportive as treatment began.

Lashing out may seem justified in the moment, but the echoes of lashing out can be devastating, making disease or suffering even more complicated than they would be all by themselves.

Prolonged Anger

Deeper still is the problem of nursing anger, letting wounds fester or nurturing one's bitterness. When one chooses this response they might bring deliberate, pre-meditated harm to others. Sometimes, though, the wounds are nursed so long it can be difficult to discover the source of the anger behind the mean-spirited action.

Clint Eastwood's artful and tragic film *Gran Torino* portrays such a person with deeply layered bitterness—a retired auto worker and widower whose neighborhood becomes a place of violence. With all that had happened to Eastwood's character, he felt justified in his crankiness, his own penchant for violence and for his deep bigotry against his neighbors. Everyone knew he was mean. No one knew why. Finding out why brought tragedy to everyone.

As we were writing this chapter, a story came to us of a pastor whose wife was diagnosed with extensive breast cancer and then bi-polar disorder after some of her behaviors that threatened his family's financial well-being came to light. In the week that the disorder was identified, this man's congregation also dismissed him without warning and without provision for severance. The leaders who initiated the dismissal felt the church was not growing enough. As hard as it is to see his way through, this pastor will need to find a way to throw himself on the hope of his faith or the seemingly justified bitterness that will grow in its place will become its own prison. And from that prison he will do to others what was done to him.

Malevolent Intent

At the bottom of this violent pit are those who plot to actively harm, torment and annihilate others.

Some find a religious motivation for malevolence, believing that those they name as apostate deserve death, and worse still, mistreatment before they die. The Spanish conquistadors, the Catholic-Protestant battles in Northern Ireland and today's ongoing and multi-faceted expressions of extreme Islamic groups provide too many graphic and gruesome examples.

For others, malevolence is economic or political or racist. Think Lenin, Stalin, Mao and Hitler. Think the Rwandan massacres, the virtual extermination of indigenous peoples and the modern resurrection of enslavement.

Malevolent intent is a source of pleasure for some. Sado-masochism may be touted as harmless decadence between consenting adults, but it is simply taking pleasure from destructive behavior, a substitution of the gross and cruel for the beautiful. Deprivation and psychological suffering is what leads someone to take pleasure in harming or being harmed, and those who participate in it extend their agony, drawing others into their orbit.

Malevolent intent can also be personal, poisonous, anti-social and unrelenting. Consider this example: on 17 April 2010, *The Milwaukee Journal Sentinel* reported on the sentencing of a young man who murdered a college student without provocation. The criminal had to be subdued when he was told he would spend life in prison. His family stood at the back of the courtroom and shouted their hatred of the victim's family because their criminal family member now had a life sentence. They had no regard for the fact the victim had been murdered. How does one even begin to address the response to suffering that willfully causes suffering in others?

Whether it is religious, political, sexual or personal, malevolent intent and its resulting devastation often starts among people who have been mistreated or feel they will be. They give themselves complete permission to inflict sorrow upon sorrow—rejoicing in it, rationalizing that what is awful has become good and reveling in their twisted successes. If they are the victorious oppressor instead of the [possibly] oppressed, then perhaps the painful ancestral or deeply psychotic memories of suffering will somehow be eased.

Inflicting when one feels there is nothing left to do

Let's return to the personal aspects of bringing harm for just a moment more. We want to point out that the agony of some who choose to harm themselves, or someone they deeply love, is because they believe it will end or relieve suffering, not because they want to cause it.

Picture a spouse of sixty wonderful years who begs you to put them out of their misery because they are terrified of the senility they feel creeping upon them. The spouse who commits murder-suicide in such an instance does so with anguish in their heart, not rage. On the surface it does not appear malevolent at all.

The problem with malevolence, though, is that it is borne from evil in general, not just the evil we intend personally. The residual evil in our world that makes disease and death comes to us all does not require us to notice it before it does its destructive work. We don't have to be conscious and actively malevolent. We swim in it. We breathe its murky air because we exist. Malevolence has its way with us whether we lash out with desire to cause harm, or whether we surrender to despair and end life with no attempt to build a platform for human achievement and tribute to God on top of our suffering.

We recently had the privilege of serving the people of First Baptist Church in Eau Claire, Wisconsin. Many in this congregation are of advanced age and have significant physical limitation. Each week it seemed we heard a new life story filled with many reasons for sorrow and defeat. Yet the people in this congregation care for one another, check on one another and are fervent in their prayers, especially the one Jesus taught us to pray:

Our Father who art in heaven,
Hallowed be Thy name.
Thy Kingdom come.
Thy will be done,
On earth as it is in heaven.
Give us this day our daily bread,
And forgive us our sins as we forgive those who sinned
against us,
And lead us not into temptation, but deliver us from
evil,
For Thine is the kingdom, and the power, and the
glory, forever.
A-men.

The very structure of this prayer stands firmly against any capacity for remaining angry or desiring harm to befall others—no matter how deep one's suffering might be.

It was a privilege to pray with these sisters and brothers in Christ as we reminded each other that it is disease and dis-ease we fight, not death.

CHAPTER 6

And now, we get all religious

One does not have to look far to find a rich set of images that teach us about transformation. The tadpole becomes a frog. The caterpillar spins a cocoon and morphs into a butterfly. The ugly duckling becomes a swan. The construction site becomes a building. The storm gives way to sunshine. A girl becomes a woman and a boy a man.

Reaching human adulthood is not just physical transformation. To become fully adult, one must be transformed *emotionally* from bawling infant to one who understands and shows appropriate expressions; *relationally* from utter dependence in order to survive to providing for others; and *spiritually* from a life alienated from one's Creator to being reconciled with God. Being reconciled with God does not just mean being at peace because one has embraced the grace God wants to give. It means a person is reconciled to the circumstances where God is with them, even in disease and suffering.

Many humans do not make it to the full flower of adulthood. Their bodies may be fully grown, but one or more of the other dimensions are undeveloped in some way. There is nothing like a family wedding to discover which adults are still little girls, still playing catty games, and which adults are little boys, still not in control of destructive impulses. Some among us remain in childhood or adolescence—not with the playfulness, innocence or naiveté that we all do well to maintain—but with the immaturity of not being aware of the effect one's speech or behavior has on others, or the long-term implications of one's conduct. Such a person can hardly be expected to manage suffering or disease very well. Or, if key relationships for a suffering person are with people stuck in a prolonged childhood, the suffering person's support system can hardly be expected to be courageous.

Growing up is a must in such circumstances. Quickly!

We watched our children transform into the full flower of adulthood earlier than many of their peers. We think this is because of Lorie's prolonged bout with disease. They saw their mother close to death. They dealt with friends who did not want to hurt beside them. They had to carry an extended anxiety about the future of their family. In such a circumstance one either overcomes (fighting disease, but not death), or they get stuck in denial, anxiety or anger. By God's grace we watched them press on and build their young adult lives in service to others. We are so grateful for this outcome instead of the many tragic turns that could have been taken. Our daughter and son are heroes to us!

The Apostle Paul has something to say about this

When the Apostle Paul wrote his letter to the Philippian church, he was in a Roman jail. Ironically, he had also been thrown in jail in Philippi while establishing its Christian community (Acts 16). The church to which he wrote started in persecution and lived under continued pressure to deny their faith. On top of this, itinerant teachers came to their church, urging them to incorporate the Law of Moses into how they practiced their Christianity—a works doctrine that made the Philippian Christians wonder if they really were Christians. From Paul's letter we also note some women in the congregation were in conflict deep enough that Paul urges others to step in and help them get along.

Because of all these troubles, Paul repeatedly urges the Philippians to finish strong, to stand firm, to continue on, to not give up, to keep going, and to see their faith journey all the way through. Paul repeats himself that often. As he nears the end of his letter (3:17-4:1), Paul describes some of the additional grace Christians are given as equipment to help their transformation along. The equipment he lists for the Philippians is available to all of us who are citizens of heaven. *And citizenship in heaven is the reason we do not need to fight death!*

Our citizenship transforms who we emulate

Paul asks the Philippians to join with others who are following his example. His Philippian audience was what is sometimes identified as a set of second generation Christians. If you are reading this book and are a follower of Jesus, you are in the third generation.

- <u>First generation:</u> Disciples who were present during the life and ministry of Jesus.
- <u>Second generation:</u> Those privileged to hear the firsthand witness of those disciples and chose to follow the Christian way.
- <u>Third generation:</u> We who embrace the gospel message recorded in the New Testament by those disciples.

It is important for those of us in this third generation to follow solid Christian examples as closely as we can. It is important that those who lead our congregations be excellent models of Christian living even as we seek to be excellent models ourselves. In this way the transformed way of life can be captured and then repeated from generation to generation.

Paul makes this a significant theme in all his writings. His letters to some of the first congregations are perhaps the most significant source Christians have for the idea of discipling—the intentional walking alongside another for the purpose of their ongoing transformation into all that God creates them to be. When there is no Christian model to follow, or if that model does not reflect the full flower of maturity, especially as ones faces suffering and eventually the loss of one's life, how does one learn to fight disease but not fear death?

Our own ability to struggle forward, in part, was because we had excellent models to follow. Our models had learned that the ultimate example to follow is Jesus Christ's approach to his own suffering and death. They taught this approach to us. As a part of this third generation of Christians, we now choose to do our best to keep the model alive.

Our citizenship transforms our perspective

Here is what the apostle Paul writes about those who embrace hostility to the cross of Christ:

> *I have often told you before and now say again even with tears, many live as enemies of the cross of Christ. Their destiny is destruction, their god is their stomach, and their glory is in their shame. Their mind is on earthly things. But our citizenship is in heaven. And we eagerly await a Savior from there, the Lord Jesus Christ....(Philippians 3:18-20 NIV).*

Here is how we express Paul's sentiment in our own words:

- They indulge hatred toward the cross. *We venerate the one who hung upon it.*
- They have a destiny, but it is one of destructiveness—the fruit of being someone who only takes and never creates. *Our destiny grows from our citizenship in heaven and our connection to the Author of Life.*

- Their god is their stomach, *but our God gives us food for which we are thankful.*
- They take glory in what should bring shame, *but we find glory in the dignity God grants to all humans through the Lord and Savior we eagerly await.*

We realize not everyone who shares a Christian identity with us shares our point of view. Some of our Christian sisters and brothers believe it appropriate to not respect the dignity of people with whom they disagree, even though the Savior they worship offers eternal hope for anyone who chooses to follow. Or, as we have noted throughout this book, their understandings about how to practice Christianity lead them to non-helpful approaches to inevitable suffering. We can only commend ourselves to those who believe and those who do not: look deeply and reflectively at Paul's words to those early Philippian believers. He explicitly reminds them that belief in life beyond the grave is the reason one strives to live at the highest and fullest level of maturity—even when faced with the most extreme circumstance. That is, *we can fight disease and dis-ease precisely because we do not need to fight death.*

Our citizenship transforms our lowly bodies

It is worth noting that resurrection without transformation would be a living hell. Why would Lorie wish to continue into eternity with more than half of her lungs missing, continued issues with Grave's disease, a nose and ears that never cease growing across the millennia, a chunk of her scalp missing and a high risk for massive blood clots? Eternal life in a body doomed to the full extent of what the Second Law of Thermodynamics offers is a terrifying prospect!

Resurrection without transformation is one way the bible describes hell. Hell is not something God inflicts as punishment, but is the result of a saving rescue that remains unclaimed. Hell is the complete absence of the divine. It is living forever with all that makes us afraid. Hell is being raised to life in one's old, untransformed body. But the power of the gospel is the promise that we will be like the Resurrected One: Jesus Christ, hope of the nations. Fear no longer has to have a hold on us.

It is this hope that we symbolize with water baptism. One enters the water and returns again, symbolizing death to sin and a resurrection for the life to come. The one who is baptized claims their citizenship in heaven, their part in the body of Christ, and their continuing transformation into the image of Christ—as one who fights all of the residual effects of darkness, including suffering, knowing that the light has already won. We can fight disease, dis-ease and be unafraid of death because God's grace has transformed us out of our fear.

When we started this book, we had no illusions it would end with a miracle. As we developed our thoughts in these pages, Lorie had to put up with two scalp surgeries, the diagnosis of Grave's disease, an old tumor that did not go away and needed to be treated by CyberKnife® all over again, and a sudden and ugly tumor removed from above her right shoulder blade that turned out to be the largest tumor to date. We are sending this manuscript to the publisher just after a new tumor showed up in a CT scan of Lorie's right lung, suspicious of metastases but as of yet too small to treat. We are in preparations for her sixteenth occurrence of battling this persistent disease.

Neither do we have grand ideas that we somehow deserve a healing that others will not know. We don't even know if Lorie will live long enough to see this book in print. Still, there are already too many miracles and gifts of grace for us to count, a grand gift of many extra days we have been able to enjoy together, and the greatest gift we have borne from the greatest miracle of all time: our faith. Whatever happens, however painful the future, we want to keep living in trust, fighting disease and welcoming life beyond the grave.

We look to the example of Paul Hiebert, a missiologist of note, who was Mark's parishioner at North Suburban Mennonite Church in Northern Illinois, near Trinity Seminary where Paul taught. When it appeared Paul's earthly life was closing out, he made arrangements to teach a brief Sunday School class on *Dying Well*, polished up his last two manuscripts, and moved to the East Coast to spend his last weeks with his children. The impact of these actions had a profound effect on his congregation, largely made up of Baby Boomers coming to terms their own aging process.

Paul Hiebert's life and light shone into the lives of many others, helping to transform their perspective about disease and death. We can only hope our story and earnest desire to live for the glory of God shines a little transformation in your direction as well.

Additional Links:

- The ProHealth Care CyberKnife® Center virtual tour:
  http://www.prohealthcare.org/services/videos/
  Cyber Knife®-center-tour.aspx

- Information about the superDimension® bronchoscopy:
  http://www.superdimension.com/view/files/Lorie
  VincentStory.pdf
  http://www.youtube.com/watch?V=XW6piIH_lyk

- The Milwaukee Journal Sentinel article after Lorie's seventh cancer occurrence:
  http://www.redorbit.com/news/health/373416/
  lorie_vincent_was_told_cancer_would_kill_her_
  in_months/

- The national advertising campaign ad on CyberKnife®, featuring Lorie's story:
  http://www.creativepd.com/unitedhemisphere
  sinsightoct08.pdf

- Lorie's ProHealth Care patient story and radio spot:
http://www.123people.com/ext/frm?ti=person%
20finder&search_term=lorie%20vincent&
search_country=US&st=person%20finder&
target_url=http%3A%2F%2Fwww.medteams.
org%2FPatients%2Fworld-classcare%2FPatient
Testimonials %2Florie-s-testimonial.aspx

(the ad is located on p.8)
- More reflections on medical outliers from *The Muse*, Mark L. Vincent's blog:
http://givingproject.wordpress.com/2010/07/
16/outliers-and-medical-justice-a-response-to-
mr-henninger/

- The website for Design Group International™:
www.DesignGroupInternational.com

ABOUT THE AUTHORS

Lorie L. Vincent was raised in Sheboygan, Wisconsin. Trained as a Christian Educator, she served the Indiana-Michigan Mennonite Conference as conference-wide minister of youth and young adults for a number of years before joining her husband Mark as founders of Design Group International™, an organizational design firm. She was diagnosed with uterine leiomyosarcoma in 1999, following a hysterectomy. She has endured sixteen occurrences of cancer in the past twelve years and is believed to be one of the longest lived people on record diagnosed with this form of leiomyosarcoma.

Mark L. Vincent, Ph.D., CCNL is a Senior Design Partner and CEO of Design Group International™, widely recognized as a lifelong student of organizational leadership, particularly where the intersection of faith and money is involved. He has lectured and written extensively on these subjects while continuing to foster new business and ministry initiatives. His blog *The Muse* and the whimsical *Whorled Viewz* cartoons from emell vee can be found at www.marklvincent.com.

Lorie and Mark resided in Northern Indiana for a number of years after having met and married while in college, moving to Lorie's home state of Wisconsin in 2001. Now that their children are raised, they divide time when Lorie is not in treatment between their families in Wisconsin, Michigan and Florida.